This book belongs to:

_____

A Jesse Tree Coloring Book:

An Advent Activity Book

A coloring book for all ages,

with daily Bible verses,

coloring pages, and ornaments

to make for your Jesse Tree.

Also by Kathleen Bagioni,

Make it Your Own Series: Straight Stole Pattern

Make it Your Own Series: Shaped Stole Pattern

Make it Your Own Series: Straight Stole with Mitered Corner Pattern

and

Hearts to God, Hands to Work:

Make It Your Own Series: Vestments and Altar Appointments

For more information, go to:

www.kdbvestments.com

A Jesse Tree Coloring Book:
An Advent Activity Book

by

Kathleen Bagioni

kdbdesigns,LLC Publishers

Tolland, CT

Published in the United States by kdbdesigns, LLC Publishers

Tolland, CT, 06084

www.kdbvestments.com

Copyright 2018 by Kathleen Bagioni, http://www.kdbvestments.com

First edition, 2018

 A Jesse Tree Coloring Book: An Advent Activity Book

Front and back cover art: Kathleen Bagioni

ISBN-13: 978-0-9600601-0-8

Registration Number, U.S. Copyright Office: TBD

Library of Congress Control Number: TBD

Printed in the United States of America

Available from Amazon.com and other fine retail outlets.

10 9 8 7 6 5 4 3 2 1

To my grandchildren,

who like to "chat-color"

with me.

I enjoy this time more than I can say.

A Jesse Tree

Let us now sing the praises of famous men,

our ancestors in their generations.

The Lord apportioned to them great glory,

His majesty from the beginning. —

Ecclesiastes 44:1-2

This is a Jesse Tree for children of all ages.

A Jesse Tree is not new.   There have been many different ideas and many ways to remember the upcoming birthday of Jesus.

A Jesse Tree Coloring Book: An Advent Activity Book has simplified Bible readings and short stories meant to be kid friendly. It is made to fit into a busy family's schedule. Coloring each day's ornament is easy to do. Maybe it will work for your family in the morning at breakfast, or while waiting for dinner in the evening, or as a quiet activity before bedtime.

Coloring book:

Each day has a brief Scripture verse to be read. There is a short story about the person in the verse. Finally, the drawing on each page represents this person or one of their famous deeds.

Ornaments to make:

On separate sheets at the rear of the book, you will find smaller scale pictures. Color and then, cut them out. Punch a hole near the top edge. String a colored ribbon through the hole. You can hang each ornament on your Jesse Tree or your Christmas tree.

Even the youngest member of the family can now participate in this simple countdown.

The Story of the Jesse Tree

A Jesse Tree is meant to be a visual depiction of Jesus' family tree. It is a collection of stories about Bible figures that came before Jesus was born.

The tradition of a Jesse Tree is an old one. It was a common motif in the medieval period. Many Old World churches are decorated with tapestries and carvings depicting Jesse Trees. Some date from the 11th century. Usually shown as a shoot or young tree growing from a sleeping or dreaming Jesse. Then the scenes progress upward to illustrate the genealogy of Jesus.

There is no limit to the number of people shown in each genealogy on the Jesse Tree. I suspect limits in early examples were due to size limits available for the artwork.

The Jesse Tree in this book has 25 entries, one for every day leading up to, and including, Christmas Day. This approximates the length of the Advent season. Start on December 1st. Some years it will fit just right, other years it will be late or early.

Other than including Jesse and ending with Jesus, there is no set list of ancestors and stories. Of course, the most famous people in the Old Testament make the most frequent appearances. And Adam, Moses, David, etc. make their appearance here, too. Also included are many women, such as, Sarah, Miriam, and Rahab. If you have a favorite Bible character or story that I have omitted, feel free to include it on **your** Jesse Tree.

There shall come forth a shoot from the stump of Jesse,

and a branch shall grow out of his roots.--

Isaiah 11:1

Day 1

A Jesse Tree

A shoot will come up from the stump of Jesse;

from his roots a Branch will bear fruit.

The Spirit of the LORD will rest on him—

the Spirit of wisdom and of understanding,

the Spirit of counsel and of might,

the Spirit of the knowledge and fear of the LORD—

Isaiah 11:1-2

When these words were written the people of Israel were not listening to God's rules. Soon a neighboring kingdom would conquer them. But God promised that even though their punishment would be hard that He would not forget them. A savior, Jesus, will come from this Jewish heritage.

These are the stories of some the men and women that were born before Jesus. Some of His ancestors were great kings, some were simple people.

But, they all did great things with the help of God.

Color your branch of the Jesse Tree.

Day 2

Adam and Eve

And he said, "Who told you that you were naked? Have you eaten from the tree that I commanded you not to eat from?" The man said, "The woman you put here with me—she gave me some fruit from the tree, and I ate it."—Genesis 3:11-12

God created the world and everything in it. It is good. We can enjoy it. We take good care of every animal, big or small, and every plant, big or small.

Adam and Eve made a mistake in the Garden of Eden. They sinned. They broke God's rules.

God punished them. He sent them away from this beautiful garden.

But, God still loved them. And God still loves us. God keeps sending people to help us live according to God's rules just like God helped the people in these stories.

What would an apple from the Garden of Eden look like?

Day 3

Noah

He (Noah) waited seven more days and again sent out the dove from the ark. When the dove returned to him in the evening, there in its beak was a freshly plucked olive leaf! Then Noah knew that the water had receded from the earth.—Genesis 8:10b-11

Time went by. People of the earth did evil things. They broke God's rule. God was angry and was going to punish them.

But Noah was a good man Noah tried to follow God's rules and God helped him. God told Noah to build a big boat, called an ark. And then, Noah gathered two of every animal.

It started to rain.Noah, and his family, and all these animals went into the ark. It rained for 40 days and nights. Noah and his family waited on the ark. All they could see was water.

Noah sent a dove out to fly all around looking for dry land. At first it did not work. Noah kept trying. Finally the dove came back with a small twig in its beak. Noah knew that the water was going away and the earth was drying up. They waited and soon they were able to step out of the ark on to dry land.

God saved Noah and his family and all the animals.

Color the dove flying back to the ark with a twig in her beak.

Day 4

Abraham and Sarah

*After this, the word of the L*ORD *came to Abram in a vision: "Do not be afraid, Abram. I am your shield, your very great reward." But Abram said, "Sovereign L*ORD*, what can you give me since I remain childless and the one who will inherit my estate is Eliezer of Damascus?" And Abram said, "You have given me no children; so a servant in my household will be my heir." Then the word of the L*ORD *came to him: "This man will not be your heir, but a son who is your own flesh and blood will be your heir." He took him outside and said, "Look up at the sky and count the stars—if indeed you can count them." Then he said to him, "So shall your offspring be. Abram believed the L*ORD*,—Genesis 15:1 - 6*

Abraham and Sarah were very rich, but they were getting old. The owned big herds of sheep and goats and camels. They had many servants. But, they did not have any children. This made them sad.

God told Abraham he would have many descendants…as many as there were stars up in the sky.

Abraham had a hard time believing this, but he trusted God.

Soon after this, Sarah had a baby boy. Sarah was 90 years old and Abraham was 100 years old when this baby was born.

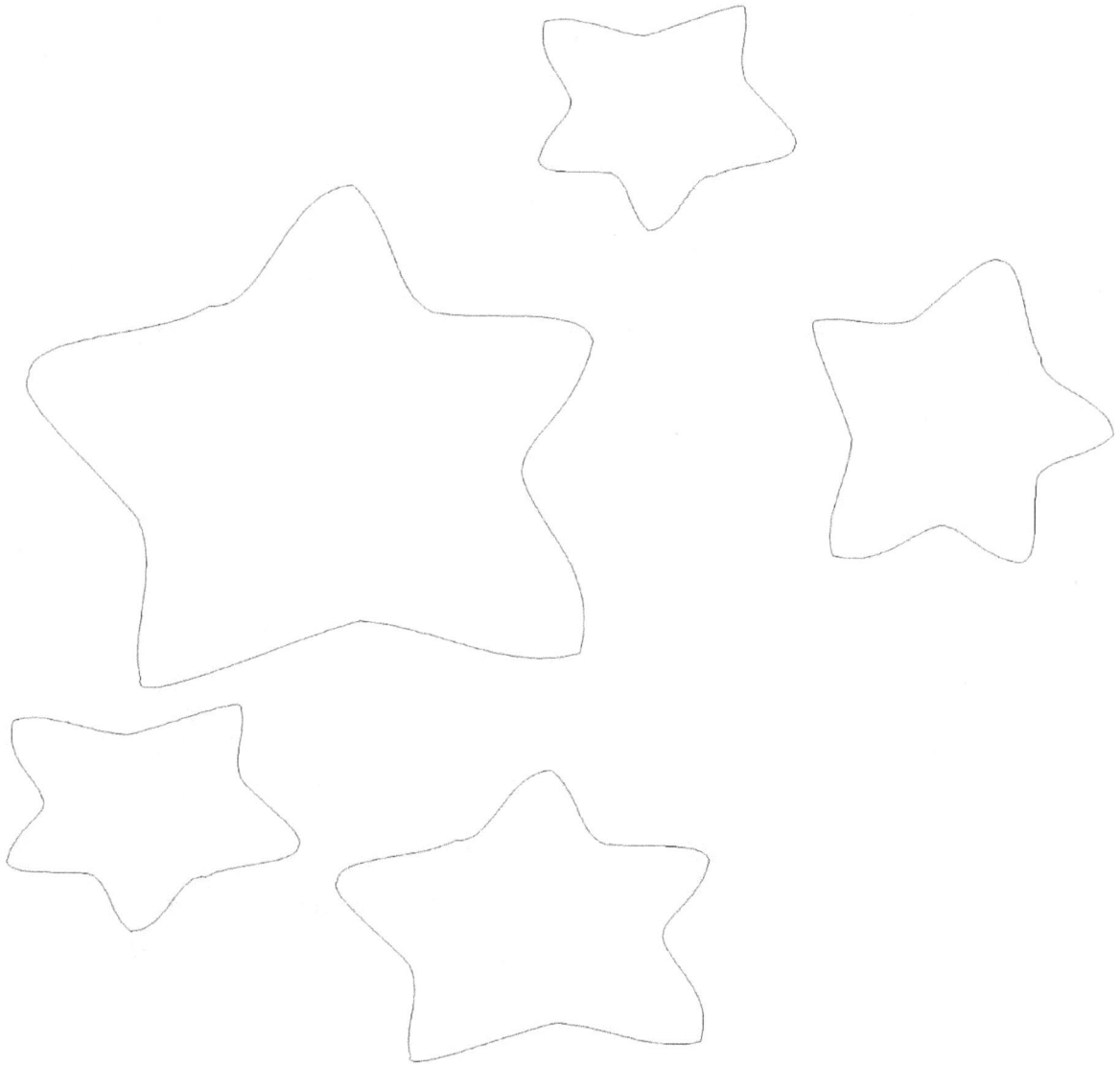

How many stars can you count in the sky at night?

Day 5

Isaac

*Sometime later God tested Abraham. He said to him, "Abraham!"
"Here I am," he replied. Then God said, "Take your son, your only
son, whom you love, Isaac, and go to the region of Moriah. Sacrifice
him there as a burnt offering on a mountain I will show you."*

*When they reached the place God had told him about, Abraham
built an altar there and arranged the wood on it. He bound his son
Isaac and laid him on the altar, on top of the wood.*

*"Do not lay a hand on the boy," (the angel) said. "Do not do
anything to him. Now I know that you fear God, because you have
not withheld from me your son, your only son."*

*Abraham looked up and there in a thicket he saw a ram caught by
its horns. He went over and took the ram and sacrificed it as a
burnt offering instead of his son.*

*So Abraham called that place The LORD Will Provide. And to this
day it is said, "On the mountain of the LORD it will be provided.—
Genesis 22:1-2, 9, 12-14*

God told Abraham he would have a son and now God says that He
will take away that son. Remember how hard it was for Abraham to
believe God? He trusted God before and now he will trust God again.

God tells Abraham to offer Isaac as a sacrifice. Abraham was sad. He
didn't understand. He and Isaac went to the top of the mountain to
obey God.

At the last moment God sent an angel to them. The angel told
Abraham where to find a ram. He could offer this ram as a sacrifice
instead of Isaac. God helped Abraham, again.

The ram's horns caught in the bushes.

Day 6

Jonah

The word of the LORD came to Jonah...“Go to the great city of Nineveh and preach against it, because its wickedness has come up before me.”

But Jonah ran away from the LORD and headed for Tarshish. He went down to Joppa where he found a ship bound for that port. After paying the fare, he went aboard and sailed for Tarshish to flee from the LORD...Then (the sailors) took Jonah and threw him overboard, and the raging sea grew calm....

Now the LORD provided a huge fish to swallow Jonah, and Jonah was in the belly of the fish three days and three nights.—Jonah 1:1-3, 15, 17

Jonah was a prophet. He promised to do God's work.

Nineveh was the capital city of a country near Israel. The Ninevites were very harsh to their enemies.

God told Jonah to go to Nineveh. But he was afraid. He did not want God to help these people. Jonah thought he could change God's plan.

But God loves all people. He even loved the fierce, cruel Ninevites. He wants all people to be good people.

God even loved Jonah when he tried to run away and hide. He helped Jonah. Jonah did not drown. He told God he was sorry and God saved him.

Then Jonah went to Nineveh. His warnings helped the Ninevites to believe in God. God spared Nineveh from destruction.

Color the big fish that swallowed Jonah.

Day 7

Jacob

He had a dream in which he saw a stairway resting on the earth, with its top reaching to heaven, and the angels of God were ascending and descending on it. – Genesis 28:12

Jacob tricked his father, Isaac. He made believe he was his older brother, Esau. His father gave him a special blessing, called the birthright blessing. This was supposed to be given to Esau. This blessing was very important in Biblical times. It meant that Esau would inherit all his father's wealth.

Jacob stole all this from his brother. And, he lied to his father.

Esau was very angry. Jacob ran away and lived far away for a long, long time.

Many years later, he had a dream. He saw angels going up and coming down from heaven on a ladder. This was a sign from God. Jacob went back home to talk to his brother again.

Esau saw Jacob and forgave him.

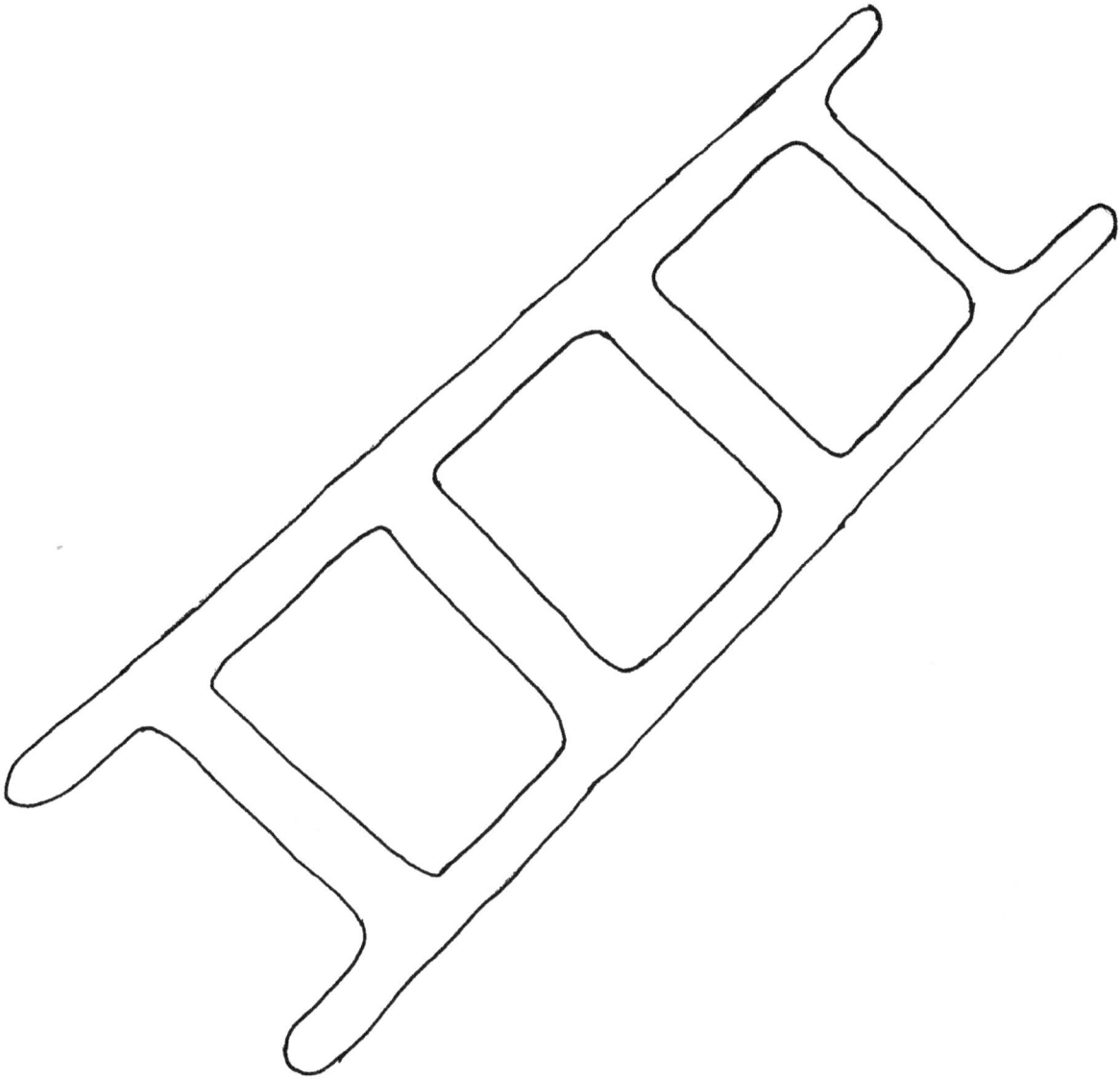

How big would a ladder have to be to reach all the way to heaven?

Day 8

Joseph

Now Israel loved Joseph more than any of his other sons because he had been born to him in his old age; and he made an ornate robe for him. When his brothers saw that their father loved him more than any of them, they hated him and could not speak a kind word to him.—Genesis 37:3-4

There were 12 brothers and one sister. But Joseph was his father's favorite. His father gave him a special gift—a very colorful coat.

This made his brothers angry and jealous. One afternoon they beat him up. They threw him into a well so he couldn't run and tell his father. The next day they sold him into slavery and Joseph was taken far away from his home.

Then, the brothers lied to their father. They told him that a wils animal killed Joseph. They showed him the special coat with blood on it.

But God helped Joseph. He became a great leader in Egypt.

Many years later there was a famine. God sent the brothers to Egypt looking for food for their family. Joseph saved them from hunger. His brothers were sorry and begged for forgiveness. The family was saved.

How many colors does your fancy coat have?

Day 9

Moses

There the angel of the LORD appeared to him in flames of fire from within a bush. Moses saw that though the bush was on fire it did not burn up. So Moses thought, "I will go over and see this strange sight—why the bush does not burn up." When the LORD saw that he had gone over to look, God called to him from within the bush, "Moses! Moses!" And Moses said, "Here I am." "Do not come any closer," God said. "Take off your sandals, for the place where you are standing is holy ground."—Exodus 3:2-5

Moses was a Hebrew boy but grew up in Pharaoh's house. Pharaoh was the king in Egypt and the Hebrews were slaves. Then Moses found out he wasn't an Egyptian but a Hebrew.

One day Moses saw a man beating a slave. He became very angry and killed the man. He ran away before he could be punished.

Many years later Moses saw a special sign from God. It was a bush that was on fire but was never burned away. God told Moses that he would be a leader. He told him to go back to Egypt.

Moses was afraid. But God helped him. Moses would bring all the Hebrew people out of slavery away from Egypt.

How many colors does fire have?

Day 10

Miriam

Then Miriam the prophet, Aaron's sister, took a timbrel (tambourine) in her hand, and all the women followed her, with timbrels and dancing. Miriam sang to them:

*"Sing to the LORD,
  for he is highly exalted.
Both horse and driver
  he has hurled into the sea." –*

Exodus 15:20-21

Miriam was Moses' big sister. Miriam was babysitting for her baby brother, Moses. She knew Hebrew baby boys were in danger. She floated him down the river in a big basket,. He floated right to the feet of the Pharaoh's sister. She adopted him.

Later when Moses became an important leader, Miriam became jealous of her "little brother". She became sick. But Moses asked God to help his sister. God healed her.

Miriam became a prophet and a musician.

Is your music loud or soft?

Day 11

Joshua

So Joshua son of Nun called the priests and said to them, "Take up the ark of the covenant of the LORD and have seven priests carry trumpets in front of it." And he ordered the army, "Advance! March around the city, with an armed guard going ahead of the ark of the LORD." —Joshua 6:6-7

Joshua was a great general of the Hebrew army. He was also a man of faith.

An angel told him to march around the enemy city with trumpets. This was a strange order for a soldier. But Joshua did what God told him to do.

All the Hebrew people marched around the city for seven days carrying the Ark of the Covenant. This was a sign that God was with them. Everyone could see this. The people in the city watched the Hebrew people blow trumpets and shout to God.

God helped the Hebrews. The walls of the great city fell down.

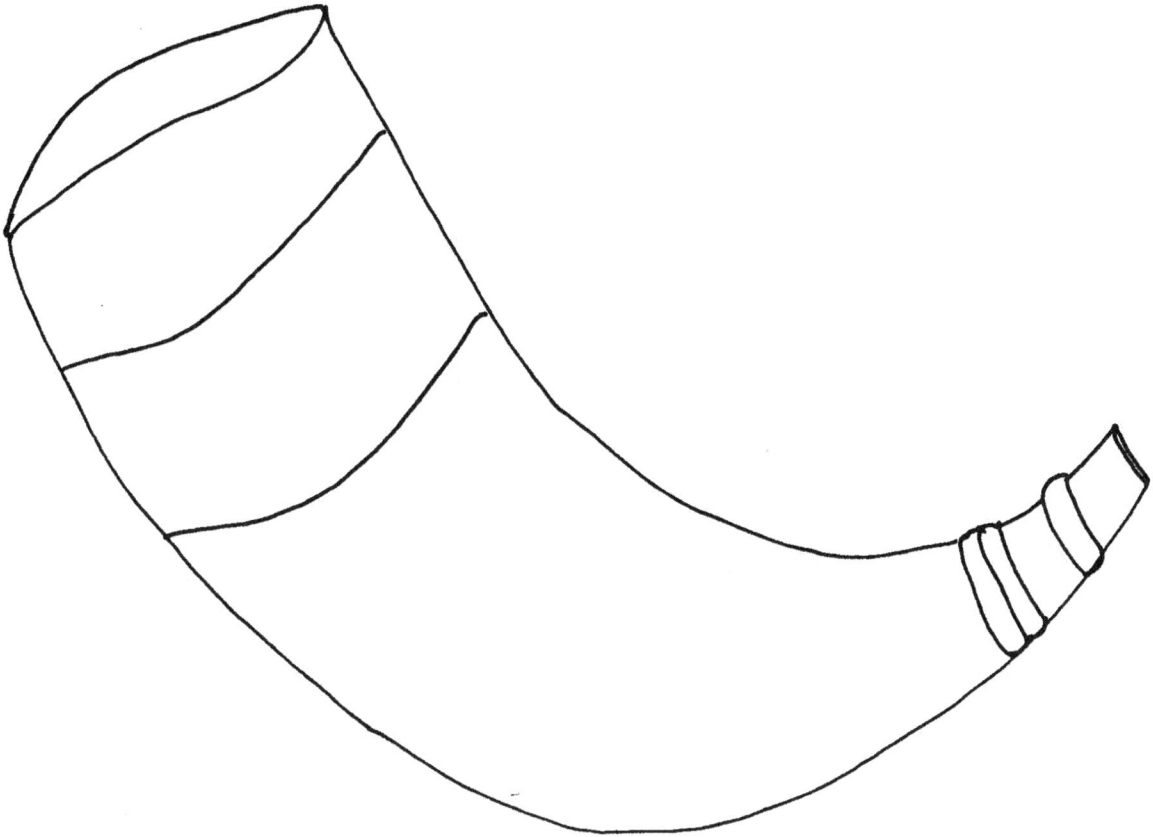

Trumpets in Joshua's time were made of ram's horns.

Day 12

Rahab

Joshua said to the two men who had spied out the land, "Go into the... (woman's) house and bring her out and all who belong to her, in accordance with your oath to her." So the young men who had done the spying went in and brought out Rahab, her father and mother, her brothers and sisters and all who belonged to her. They brought out her entire family and put them in a place outside the camp of Israel.— Joshua 6:22-23

Rahab was a woman living in Jericho.

Why did she help the spies of Joshua? It was dangerous to help strangers. But she saw how the Israelites trusted God. She saw how God helped them.

She wanted to be on the side of God. She was not a Hebrew but she had a deep faith in God.

Her courage and faith saved her and her entire family.

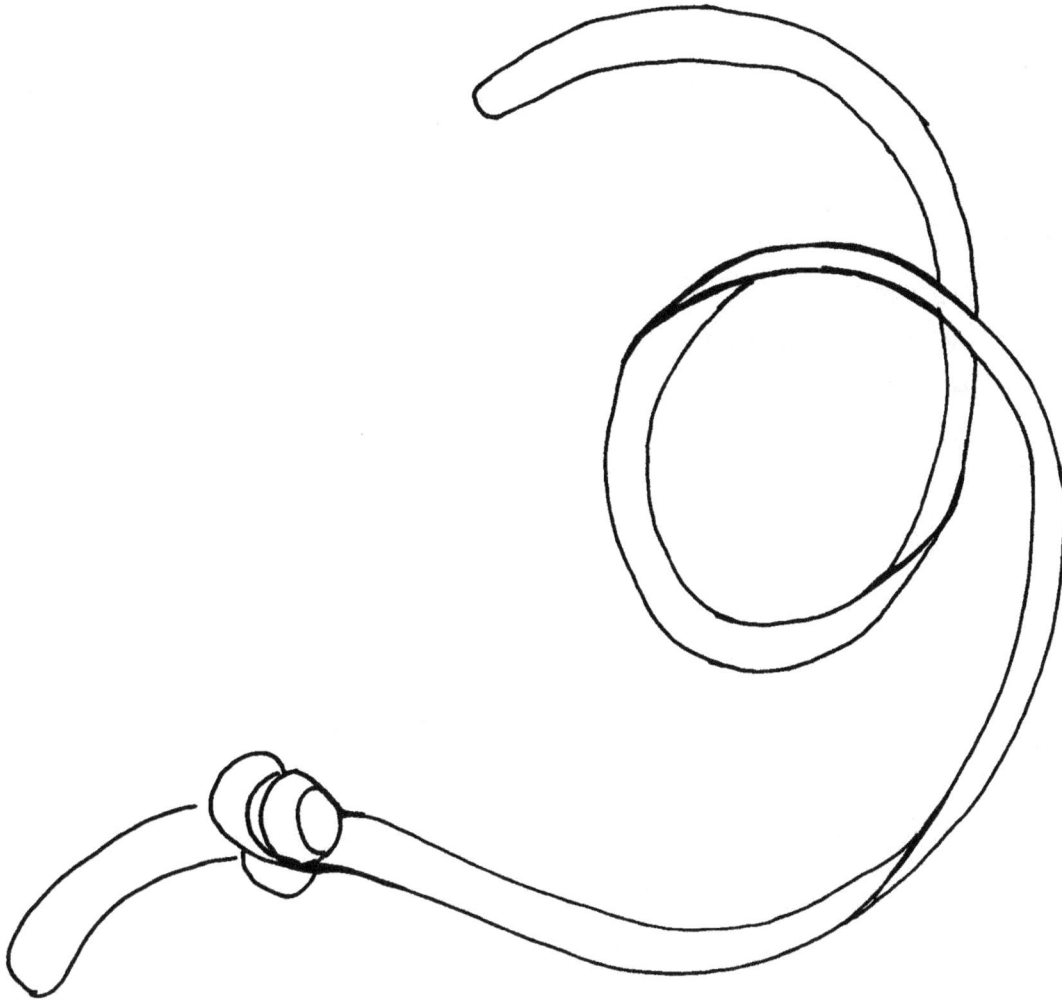

Rahab used a rope to help Joshua's men sneak in the enemy city by climbing in a window.

Day 13

Deborah

Now Deborah, a prophet, the wife of Lappidoth, was leading Israel at that time. She held court under the Palm of Deborah between Ramah and Bethel in the hill country of Ephraim, and the Israelites went up to her to have their disputes decided.—*Judges 4:4-5*

Deborah was the only woman we know that was a judge. Judges were the leaders of Israel before there were kings. She was also a prophet and a song writer.

Deborah was not only a wise judge but also a courageous leader in battle.

The Hebrew people were a conquered people again. But they did not forget God and continued to pray and follow his rules.

Deborah held court outside under the shade of palm trees.

Day 14

Ruth

But Ruth replied, "Don't urge me to leave you or to turn back from you. Where you go I will go, and where you stay I will stay. Your people will be my people and your God my God. Where you die I will die, and there I will be buried. May the LORD deal with me, be it ever so severely, if even death separates you and me." When Naomi realized that Ruth was determined to go with her, she stopped urging her.—Ruth 1:16-17

Ruth's husband had died but she stayed with her husband's family. Now, her father-in-law was also dead. It was only Ruth and her mother-in-law, Naomi. Life for two widows was very hard.

Naomi, told her to go back home to her own family. She would be safe with them. But Ruth would not leave Naomi. She believed God would help them.

The women worked together to glean in the fields to get enough food to eat. This meant they spent hours, bent over, picking up little grains of wheat from the ground. It was hard, back-breaking work.

People saw Ruth's kindness and loyalty to Naomi.

Later, she is rewarded.

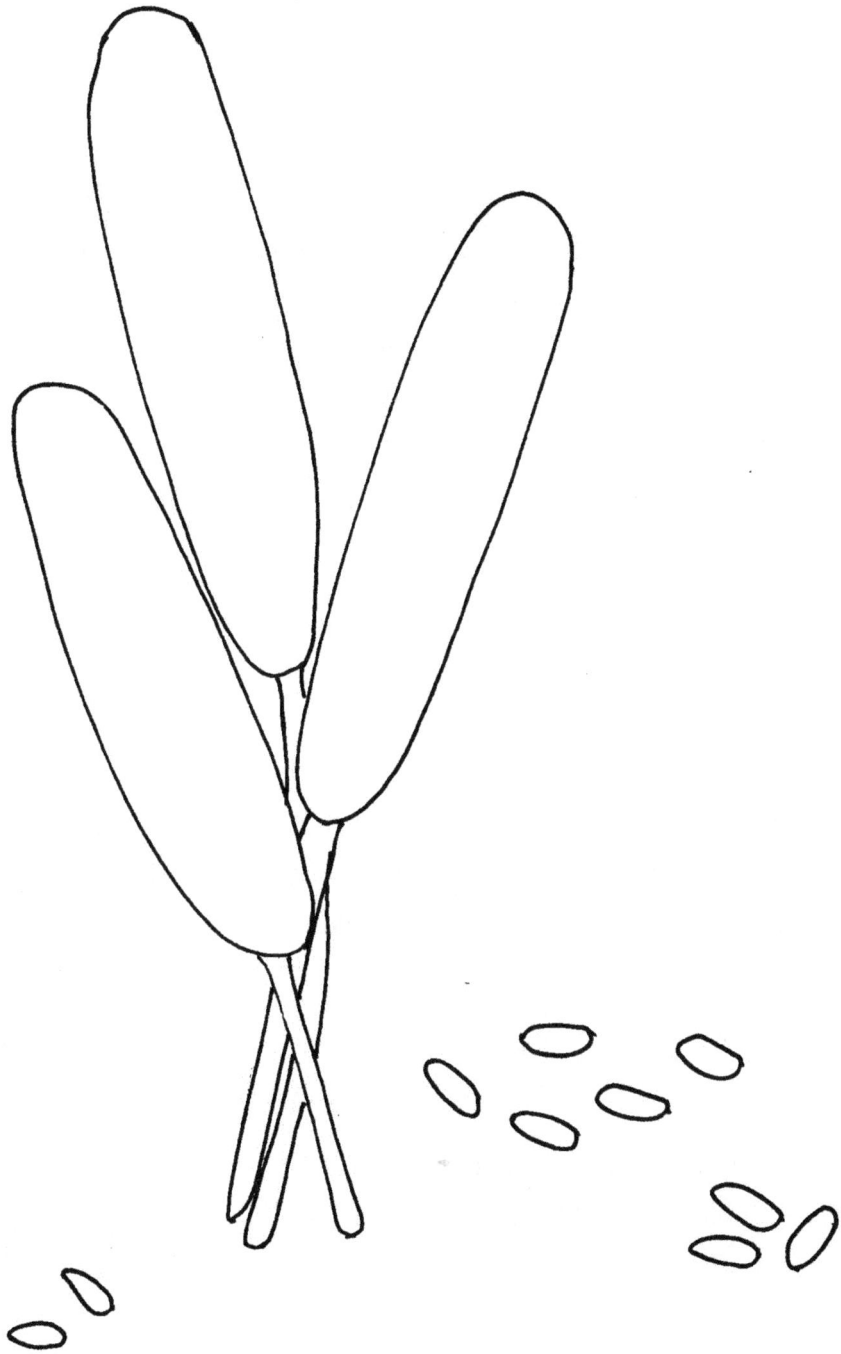

How long do you think it would take to pick up all the grains of wheat to make one loaf of bread?

Day 15

Samuel

The LORD was with Samuel as he grew up, and he let none of Samuel's words fall to the ground. And all Israel from Dan to Beersheba recognized that Samuel was attested as a prophet of the LORD.—
1 Samuel 3:19-20

Samuel's parents brought him to live in the temple when he was about three years old. He grew up there. He worked as a servant and helper to the priests that also lived and worked there. He learned from them from the time he was very little.

This was not the only reason that Samuel became a great leader. He chose to follow God's plan.

It is Samuel who anoints the first king of Israel. Anointing is a special blessing. Holy oil is put on the head of a person. This shows the people that God wants this person to be their leader.

Color Samuel's jar of sacred oil and the king's crown.

Day 16

David

But the LORD said to Samuel, "Do not consider his appearance or his height, for I have rejected him. The LORD does not look at the things people look at. People look at the outward appearance, but the LORD looks at the heart."… Jesse had seven of his sons pass before Samuel, but Samuel said to him, "The LORD has not chosen these." So he asked Jesse, "Are these all the sons you have?" "There is still the youngest," Jesse answered. "He is tending the sheep." Samuel said, "Send for him; we will not sit down until he arrives." So he sent for him and had him brought in. He was glowing with health and had a fine appearance and handsome features.—1 Samuel 16:7, 10-12

God sent Samuel on a mission… find and anoint the next king of Israel.

Jesse had eight sons. Some looked like a very good choice to be king. Some were strong-looking, some were tall. But God does not care what we look like. God told Samuel these were not the right men. Jesse had one more son, but he was not at home.

David was the youngest son, only a boy. He working in the fields taking care of his father's flock. He was a shepherd.

God knew best.

Samuel waited until David came back to the house. He anointed him king of Israel. David would become a great king.

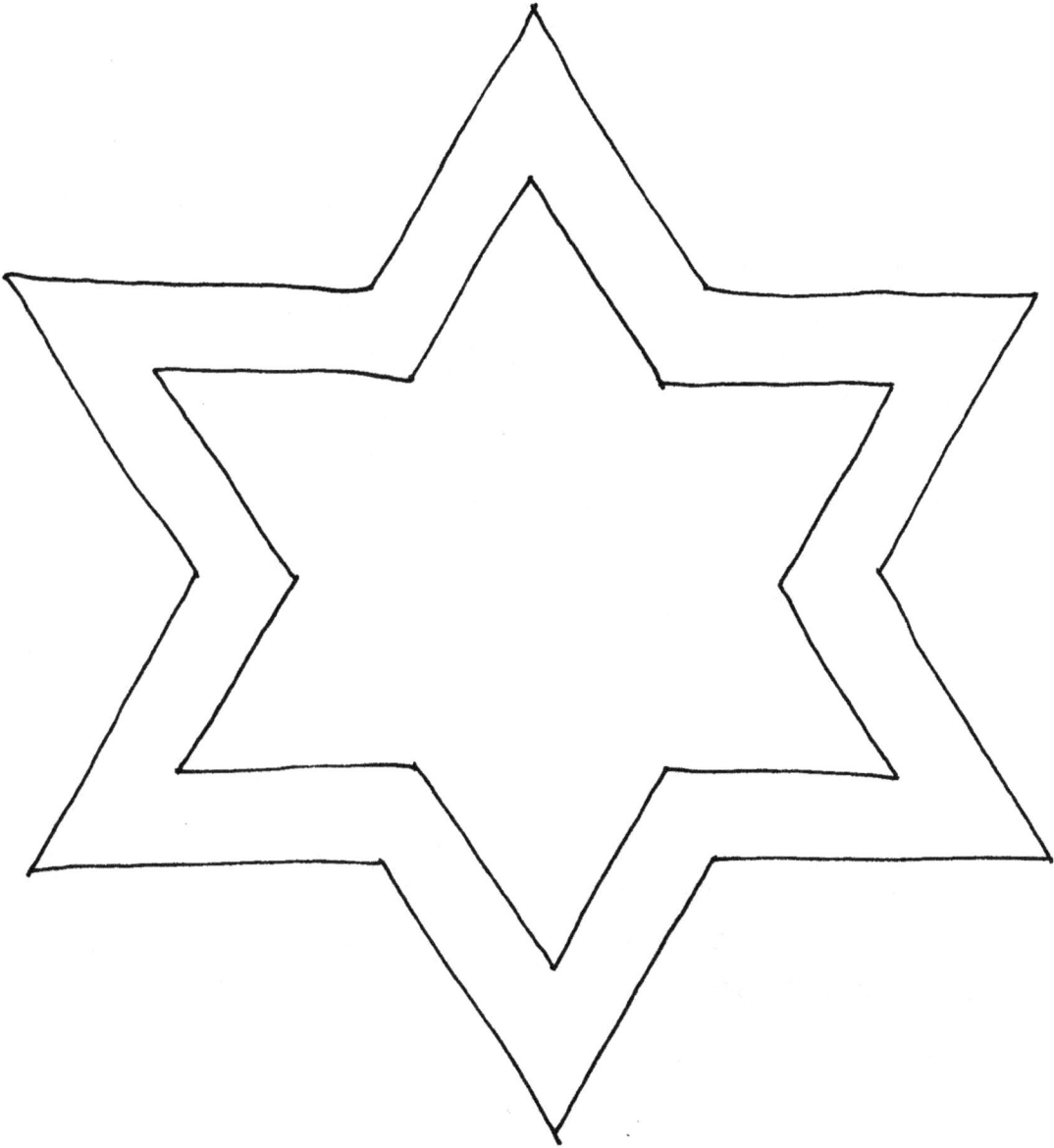

People still use the Star of David. King David is still remembered today.

Day 17

Solomon

"Now, LORD my God, you have made your servant king in place of my father David. But I am only a little child and do not know how to carry out my duties. Your servant is here among the people you have chosen, a great people, too numerous to count or number. So give your servant a discerning heart to govern your people and to distinguish between right and wrong. For who is able to govern this great people of yours?"—I Kings 3:7-8

Solomon was the wisest man that ever lived. He did not ask for riches or long life. He asked God for the gift of wisdom. This request pleased God. Solomon wanted to use his gift to help his people.

Solomon built a new temple to God. He dedicated this temple to the worship of God.

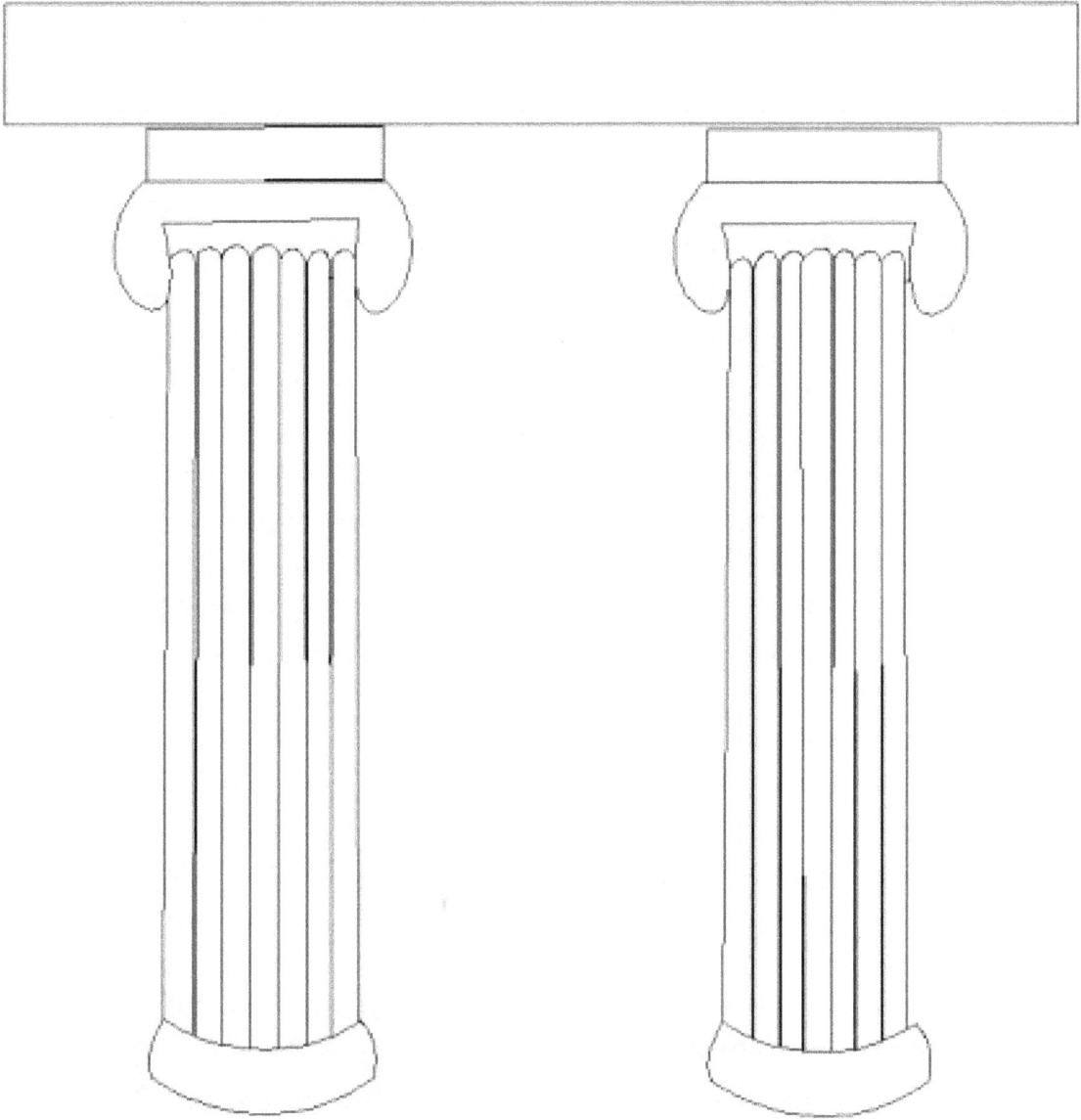

King David designed the temple but his son,

King Solomon built it.

Day 18

Elijah

As they were walking along and talking together, suddenly a chariot of fire and horses of fire appeared and separated the two of them, and Elijah went up to heaven in a whirlwind. Elisha saw this and cried out, "My father! My father! The chariots and horsemen of Israel!"—2 Kings 2:11-12a

Elijah was not a popular prophet. He did not make it easy for people if they did wrong. He was only interested in God's work not what people said about him.

He once confronted 450 false prophets, all at the same time. These prophets did not worship God. God showed his power and all the false prophets died. Then the evil king was angry that all his prophets were dead. The king wanted to kill Elijah.

God protected Elijah from the king. He brought Elijah to heaven in a golden chariot.

Color this chariot of fire.

Day 19

Isaiah

Hear me, you heavens! Listen, earth!
  For the LORD has spoken:
"I reared children and brought them up,
  but they have rebelled against me.
The ox knows its master,
  the donkey its owner's manger,
but Israel does not know,
  my people do not understand."

Woe to the sinful nation,
  a people whose guilt is great,
a brood of evildoers,
  children given to corruption!
They have forsaken the LORD;
  they have spurned the Holy One of Israel
  and turned their backs on him.—Isaiah
1:2-4

Isaiah was the greatest prophet of Israel.

Isaiah has a job in the temple as a scribe. Later God called him to another job, to be a prophet.

God warned Isaiah that most of the people would not listen to him. But God wanted to help them and give them a chance.

Some people did listen to Isaiah. They were brought back to God.

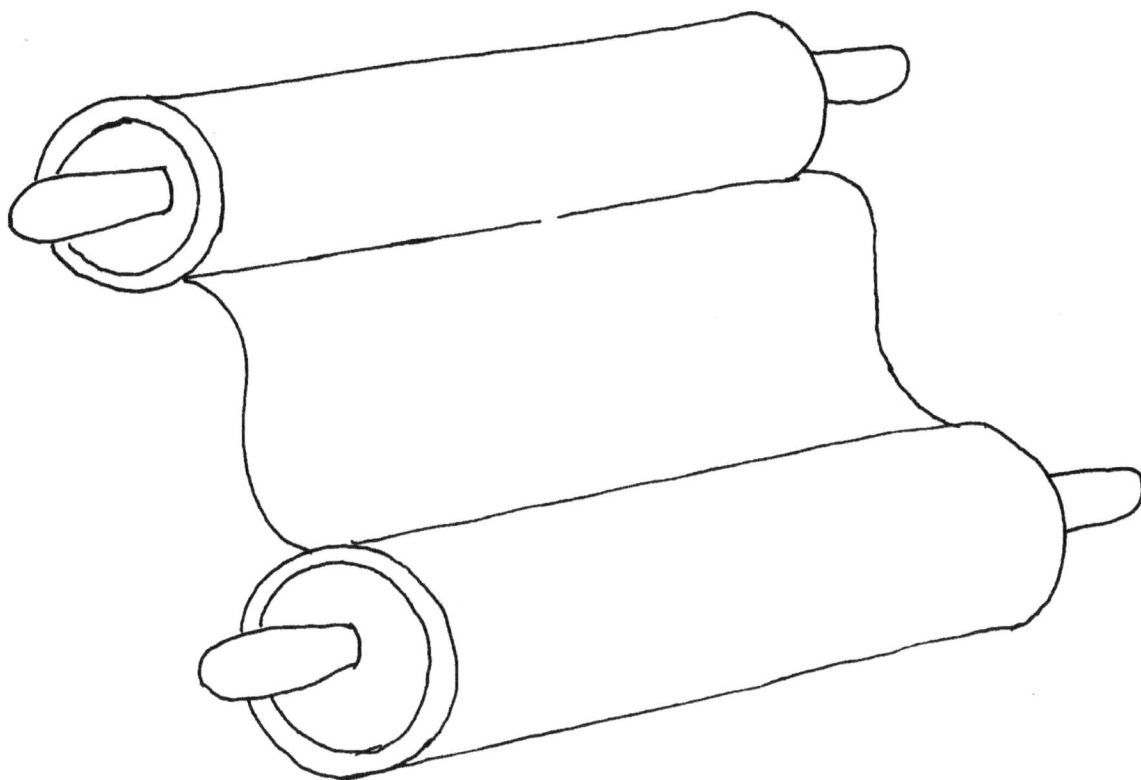

The words of the prophets, like Isaiah,
were written on scrolls.

Day 20

Elizabeth and Zechariah

When Elizabeth heard Mary's greeting, the baby leaped in her womb, and Elizabeth was filled with the Holy Spirit. In a loud voice she exclaimed: "Blessed are you among women, and blessed is the child you will bear! But why am I so favored, that the mother of my Lord should come to me? As soon as the sound of your greeting reached my ears, the baby in my womb leaped for joy. Blessed is she who has believed that the Lord would fulfill his promises to her!"—Luke 1:41-45

Mary was going to have a baby and she wanted to tell her family. Elizabeth was Mary's cousin. She was going to have a baby, too.

When an angel first told Elizabeth's husband, Zechariah, they were going to have a baby he was surprised. He did not believe the good news at first. God made him mute, unable to talk. He was not able to speak again until the baby was born.

This baby was John the Baptist.

People knew a wonderful thing was going to happen, even before Jesus was born.

Elizabeth was Mary's cousin. Zechariah was her husband.

Day 21

John the Baptist

He went into all the country around the Jordan,
preaching a baptism of repentance for the forgiveness
of sins. As it is written in the book of the words of
Isaiah the prophet:

"A voice of one calling in the wilderness,
'Prepare the way for the Lord,
  make straight paths for him.
Every valley shall be filled in,
  every mountain and hill made low.
The crooked roads shall become straight,
  the rough ways smooth.
And all people will see God's salvation.'" – Luke 3:3-6

John the Baptist repeats the words of the great prophet, Isaiah about the coming Messiah.

John was on the banks of the river Jordan baptizing people. This was a sign that they wanted to get close to God.

Later, Jesus will come to John to be baptized before he begins his public ministry. John is surprised. He says that Jesus should be baptizing him.

John knew that Jesus was the Messiah promised in the Scriptures.

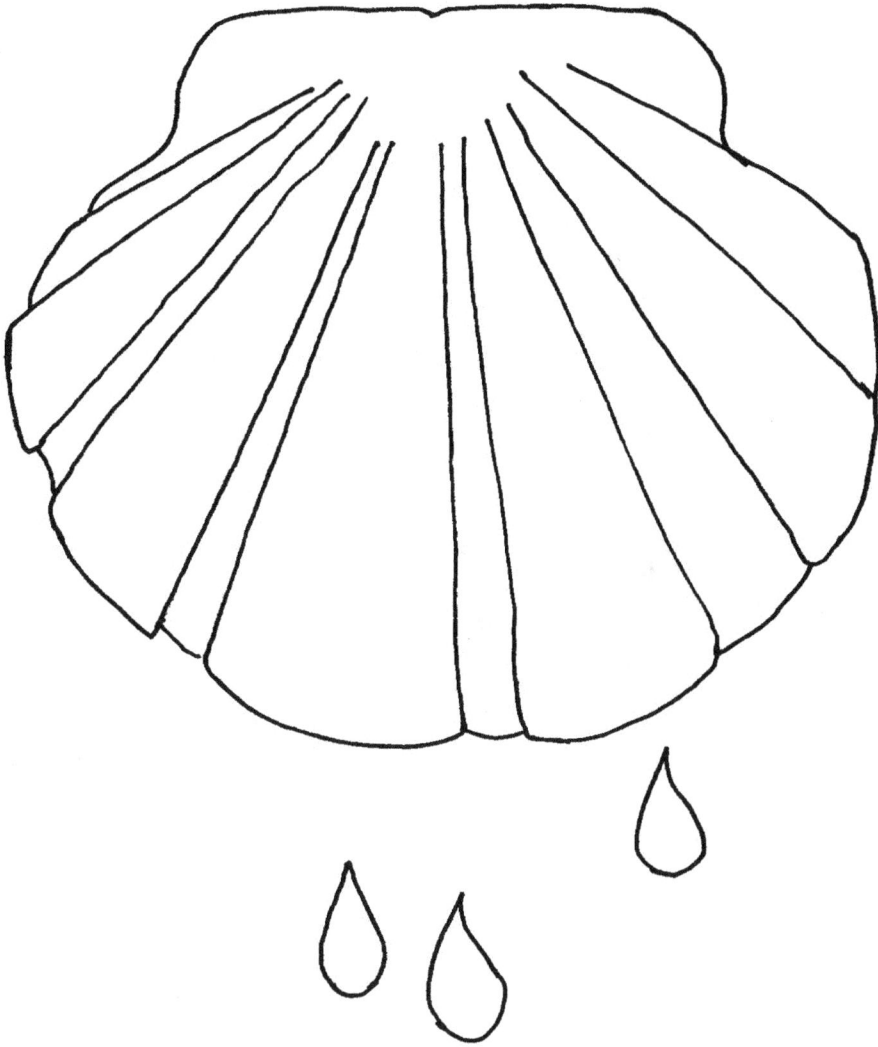

The scallop shell is a common symbol for baptism.

Day 22

Mary

In the sixth month of Elizabeth's pregnancy, God sent the angel Gabriel to Nazareth, a town in Galilee, to a virgin pledged to be married to a man named Joseph, a descendant of David. The virgin's name was Mary. The angel went to her and said, "Greetings, you who are highly favored! The Lord is with you."

Mary was greatly troubled at his words and wondered what kind of greeting this might be. But the angel said to her, "Do not be afraid, Mary; you have found favor with God. You will conceive and give birth to a son, and you are to call him Jesus. – Luke 1: 26-31

Mary was only 14 or 15 when she met this angel. She was a teenager when she said "yes" to God's plan.

It was hard for an unmarried girl to tell her family and friends that God told her she was going to have a baby.

Would they believe her?

She was engaged to marry a young man, named Joseph.

Would he believe her?

Would he help her?

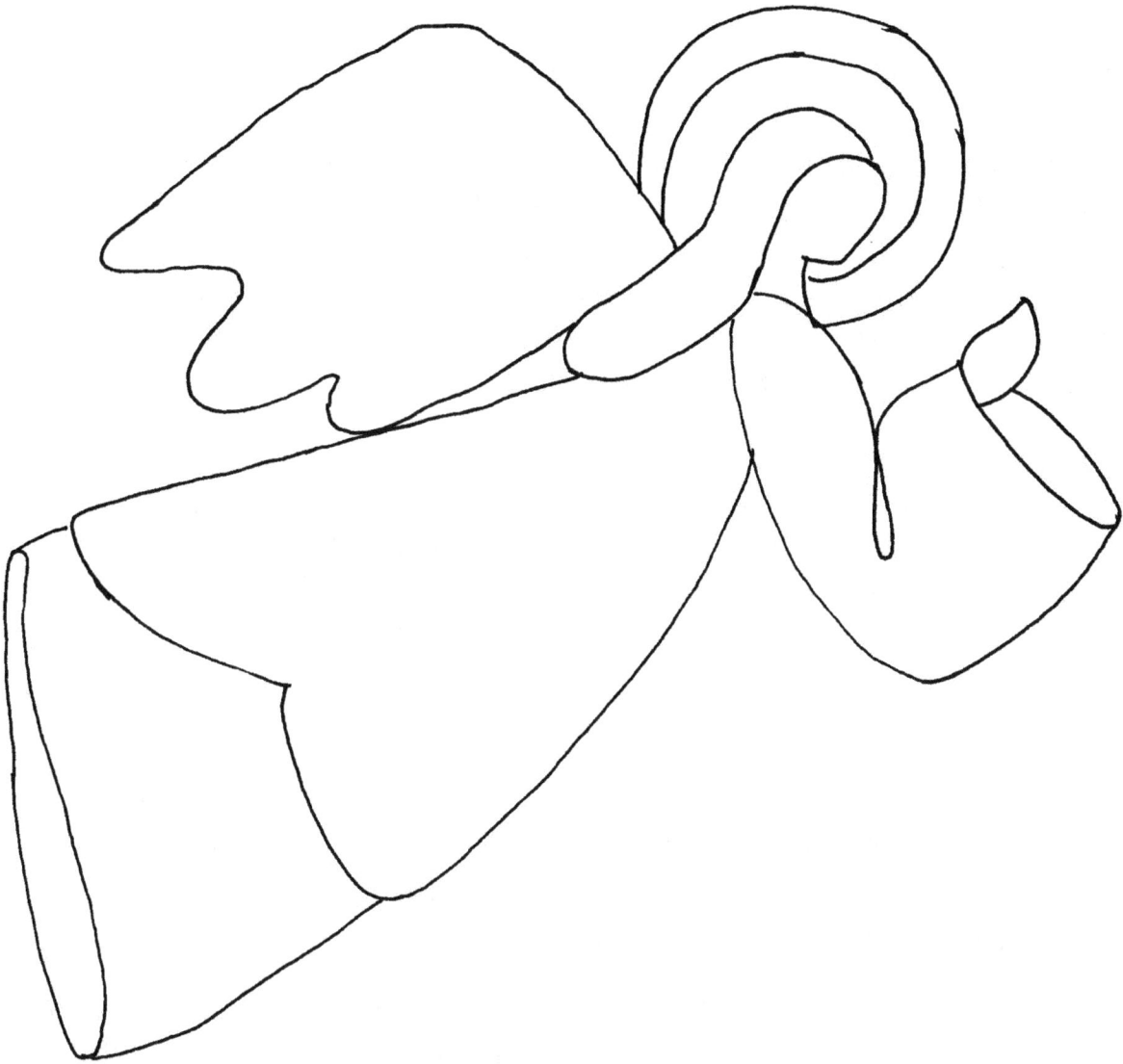

Mary was afraid but still said "yes" to God. An angel told her of God's plan for her.

Day 23

Joseph

This is how the birth of Jesus the Messiah came about: His mother Mary was pledged to be married to Joseph, but before they came together, she was found to be pregnant through the Holy Spirit. Because Joseph her husband was faithful to the law, and yet did not want to expose her to public disgrace, he had in mind to divorce her quietly.

But after he had considered this, an angel of the Lord appeared to him in a dream and said, "Joseph son of David, do not be afraid to take Mary home as your wife, because what is conceived in her is from the Holy Spirit. She will give birth to a son, and you are to give him the name Jesus, because he will save his people from their sins."—Matthew 1:18-21

Joseph loved Mary. He had asked her to marry him. They were engaged. Then an angel came to talk to Mary. She was going to have a baby.

Joseph was a good man. He did not want to hurt Mary. The law at that time were very harsh. Joseph could call off the wedding. Mary could even be put to death.

God sent an angel to talk to Joseph. He comforted Joseph. God told him to help Mary.

Her child was going to be Jesus.

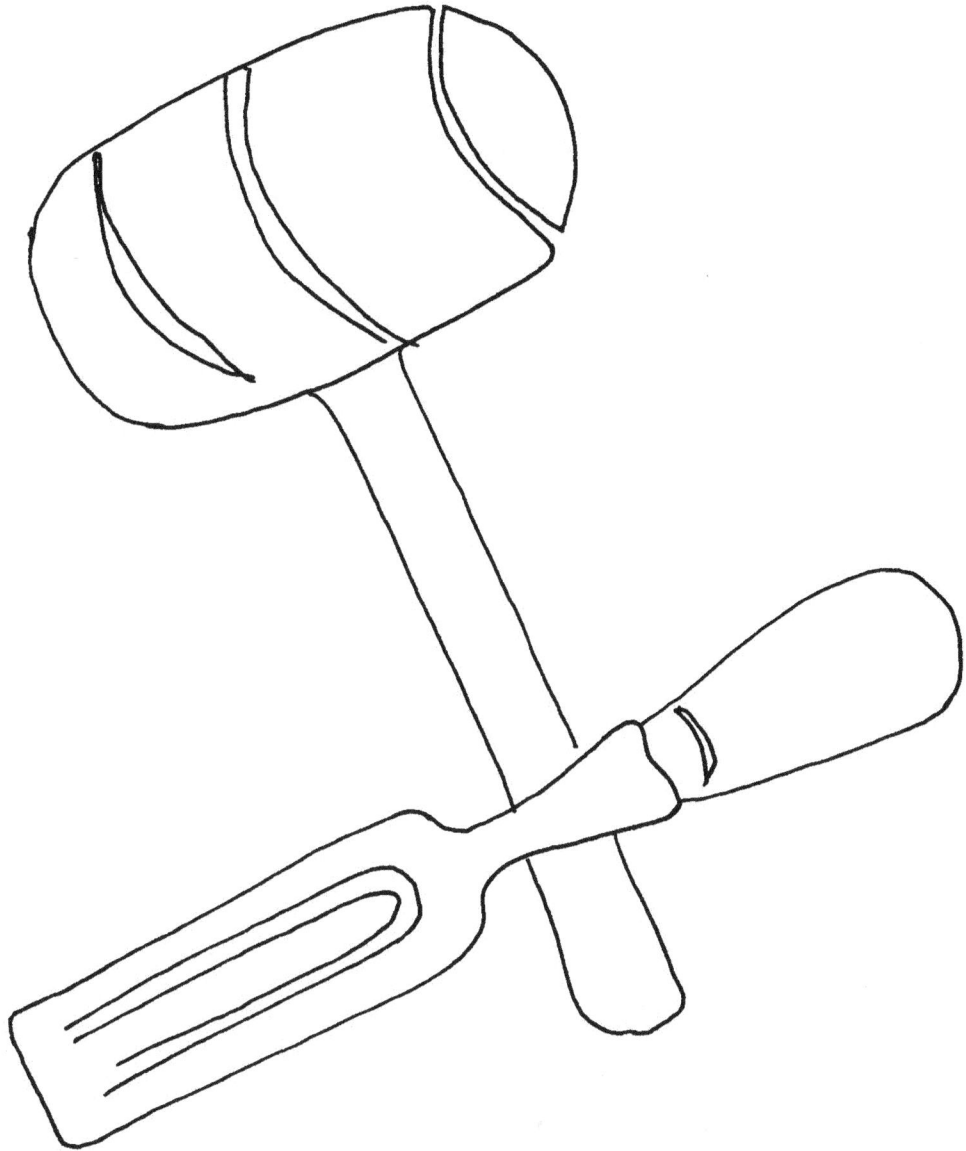

Joseph was a carpenter. When Jesus was a boy, he helped him in his shop.

Day 24

Jesus

In those days Caesar Augustus issued a decree that a census should be taken of the entire Roman world. (This was the first census that took place while Quirinius was governor of Syria.) And everyone went to their own town to register.

So Joseph also went up from the town of Nazareth in Galilee to Judea, to Bethlehem the town of David, because he belonged to the house and line of David. He went there to register with Mary, who was pledged to be married to him and was expecting a child. While they were there, the time came for the baby to be born, and she gave birth to her firstborn, a son. She wrapped him in cloths and placed him in a manger, because there was no guest room available for them.—Luke 1:1-7

A Roman decree was an order. You had to obey it. If you did not, you could be punished.

Joseph and Mary had to register. They had to travel from Nazareth to Bethlehem. In a car this would take us less than two hours in a car. But Joseph and Mary had to walk. And, Mary was almost ready to have her baby. It was very hard for her. Joseph helped but it took them a long time. Some people say it took them a week.

There were a lot of people were traveling at the same time to register. There were a lot of people in Bethlehem and no rooms for Joseph and Mary. A kind innkeeper helped them. He let them stay in the stable with the animals.

When Jesus was born he was wrapped in clean cloths and laid in a manger.

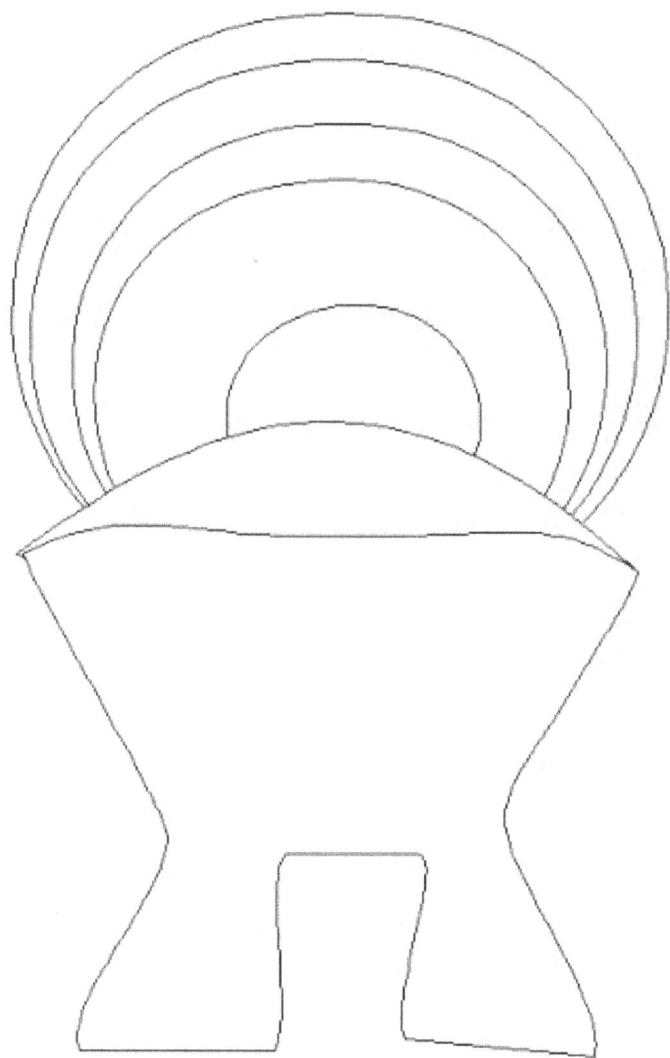

A manger can be a big box made of wood, or a carved out bowl in a rock. Food is put in the manger for the animals to eat.

Day 25

Jesus is born

For to us a child is born,
to us a son is given,
and the government will be on his shoulders.
And he will be called
Wonderful Counselor, Mighty God,
Everlasting Father, Prince of Peace.
Of the greatness of his government and peace
there will be no end.
He will reign on David's throne
and over his kingdom,
establishing and upholding it
with justice and righteousness
from that time on and forever.—Isaiah 9:6-7

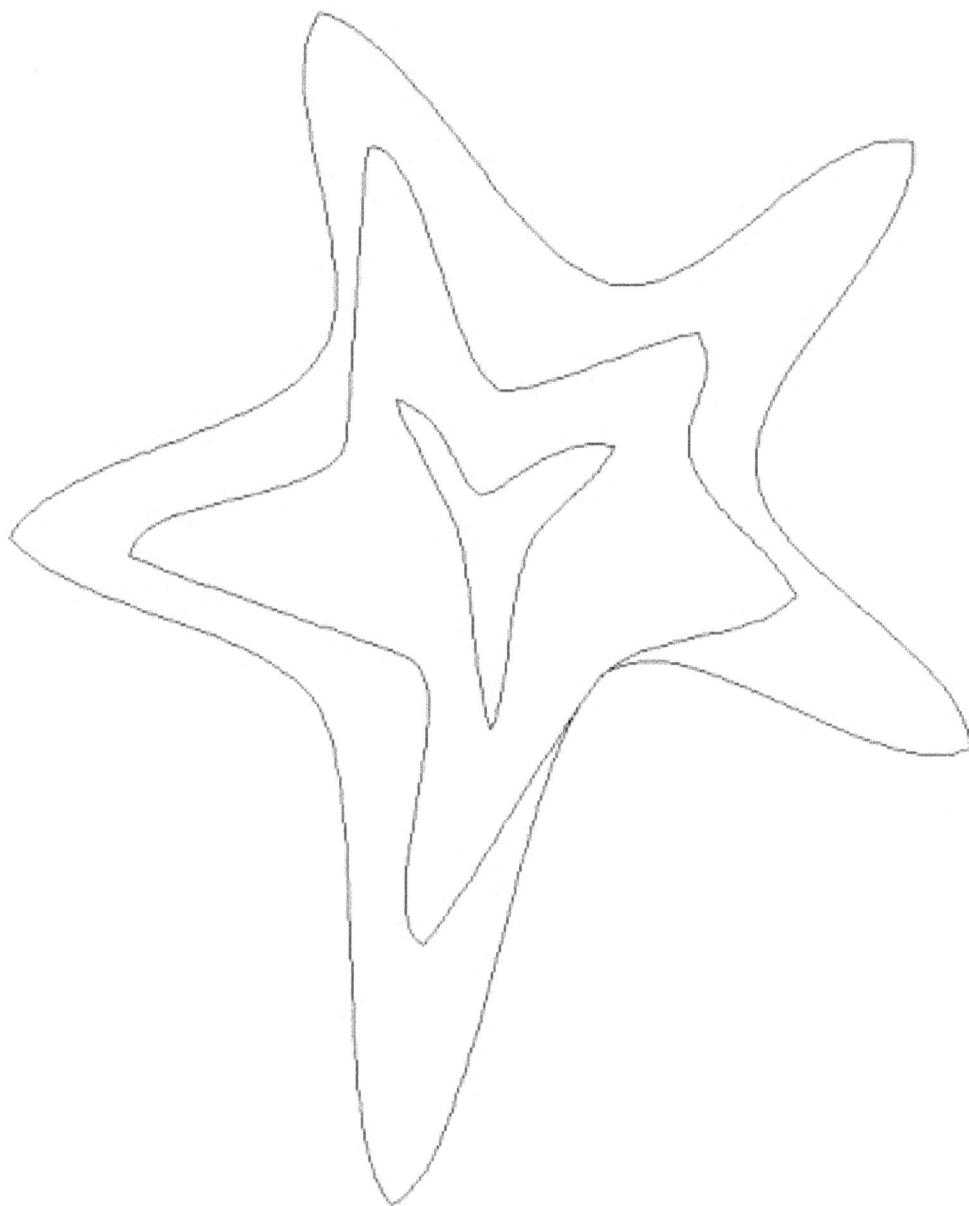

The Christmas star was so special that three wise men from far away to saw it.

Color these pictures. Cut out around the circle. Make one hole near the top of the circle with a paper punch. Thread a 6 inch length of colored yarn or ribbon through the hole. Hang on your Jesse Tree.

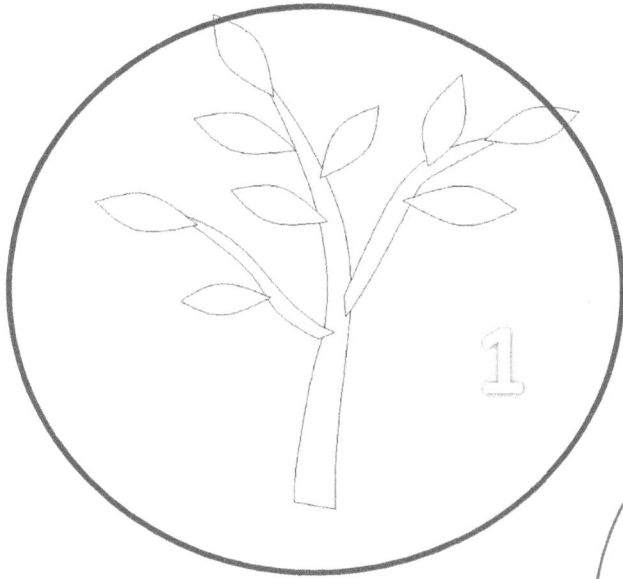

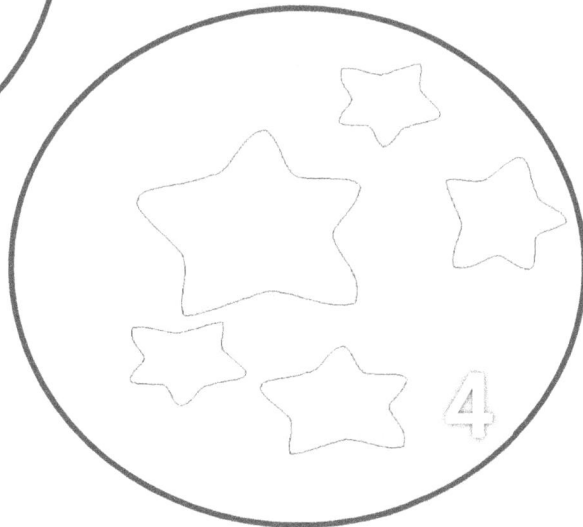

1

2

3

4

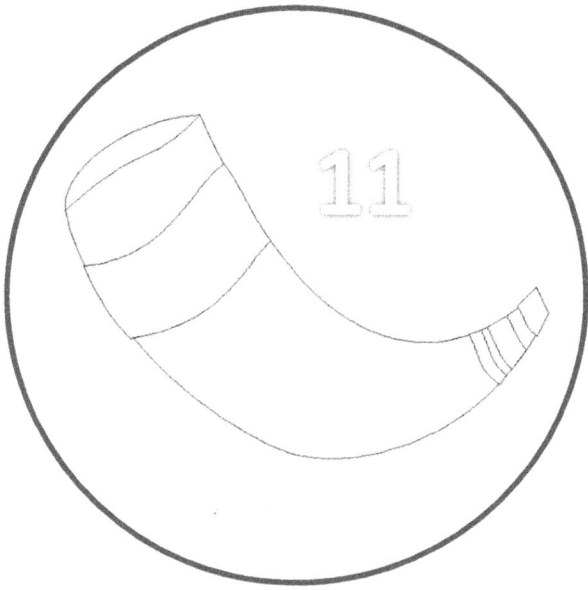

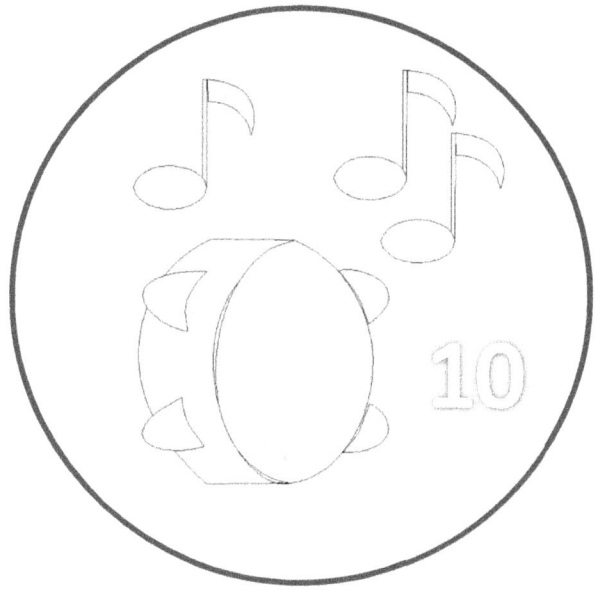

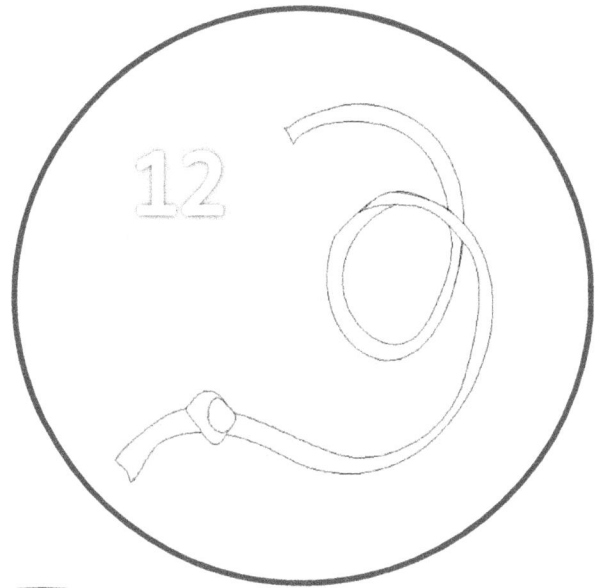

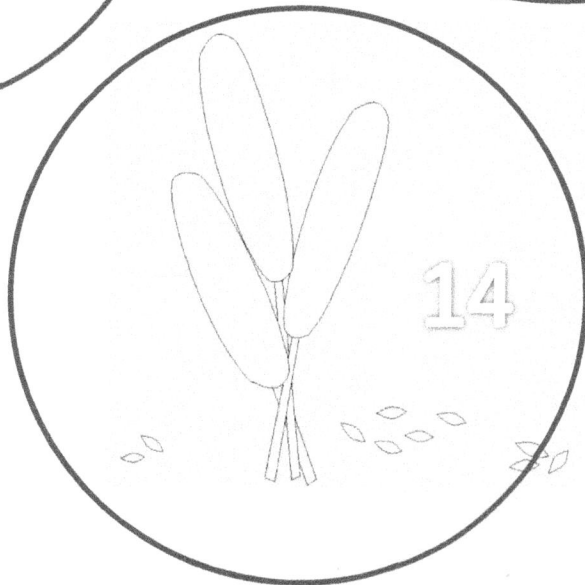

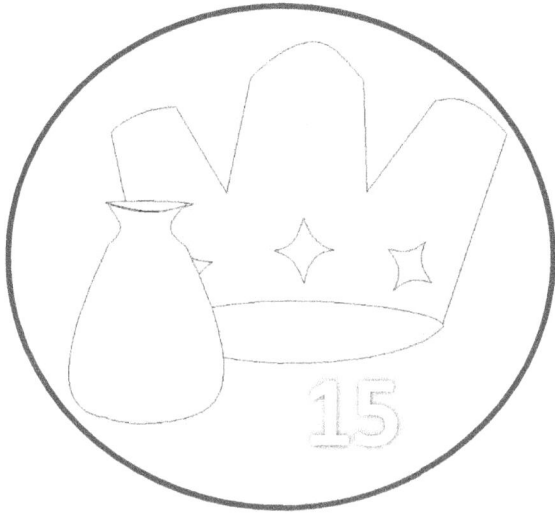

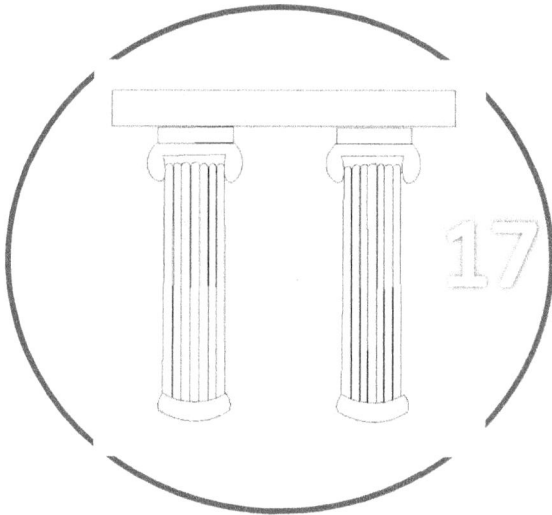

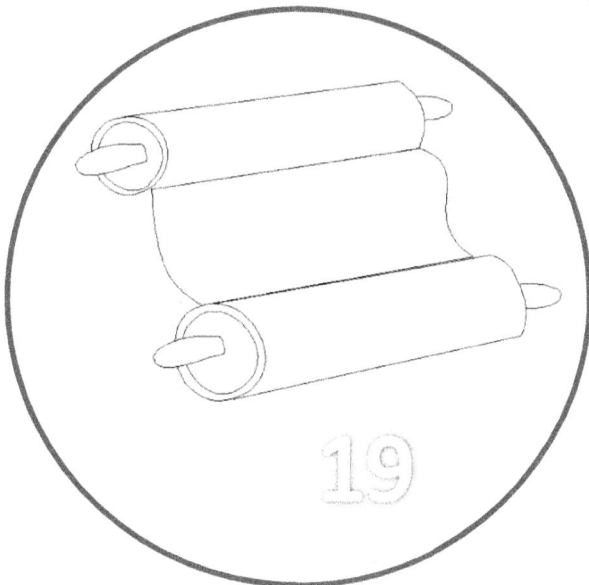

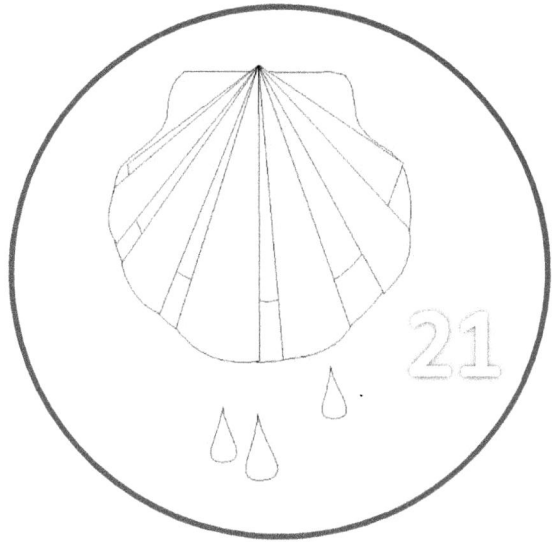

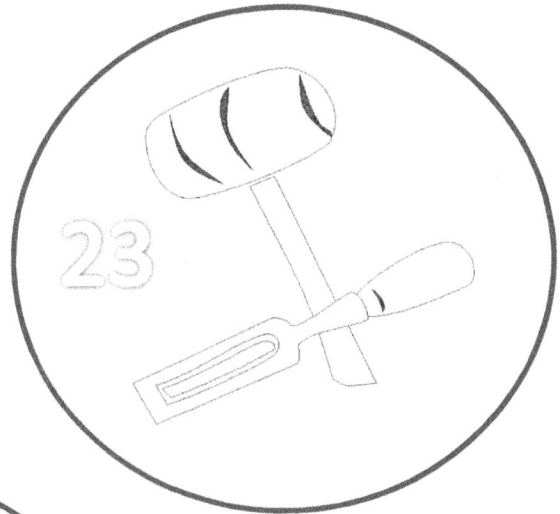

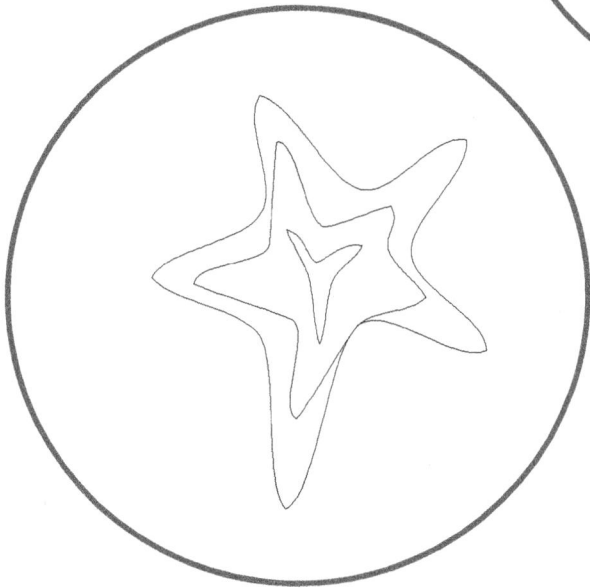

www.ingramcontent.com/pod-product-compliance
Lightning Source LLC
Chambersburg PA
CBHW081222020426
42331CB00012B/3072